Cub Scout Songbook

BOY SCOUTS OF AMERICA

Contents

Copyright © 1969
BOY SCOUTS OF AMERICA
North Brunswick, New Jersey

Library of Congress
Catalog Card Number: 73-91455
ISBN 0-8395-3222-9

No. 3222   48M177

Hints for Song Leaders

id you ever see someone get up in ront of a group and say something ke this: "Now we're all going to sing lome on the Range'—ready, sing!"? e probably wondered why everybody arted at different times in different eys—or didn't start at all.

inging is fun. Leading and teaching ongs can be fun, too. But there are ertain sensible rules a song leader ust follow. These rules aren't ifficult. You don't have to sing like Caruso or wave a baton like Toscanini to lead songs well. Many top song leaders are only average singers themselves, and many get excellent results with a minimum of arm motion. So can you. Here are some tips:

SONG LEADING

1. Smile at your group. Relax. Radiate confidence and enthusiasm, even if you don't feel particularly confident or enthusiastic. Morale is catching.

2. Tell 'em the name of the song they're going to sing. Always start with a rousing, well-known "warm-up" number, so everybody, including you, can sing out with confidence.

3. Be sure to give the pitch. Sing a few bars yourself or have a couple of bars played, if an instrument is available.

4. Start the singing with a slight upward arm motion, then a decisive downward motion (a downbeat) and begin singing yourself. Don't worry if some don't start with the first note—they'll join in quickly.

5. Beat time with a simple up-and-down motion of the arm—but make it definite and brisk. You're in command. In songs whose time is 2/4, 3/4, or 6/8, make the downbeat on the first beat of each measure. In songs with 4/4 time, make downbeats on the first and third beats.

6. Control volume by raising your hands for loudness, lowering them for softness.

7. Move around a little, inject a little pep and personality. Keep smiling.

8. Spark enthusiasm by dividing the crowd for a song or two. Groups sing separately or when you point to them, then all together. Vary straight singing with occasional humming, whispering, or rhythm clapping.

9. Stop before you're stopped. Leave them wanting more; not glad that you left.

TEACHING A SONG

Teaching a song is a part of song leading itself, so all the above rules apply. Teaching offers some special problems, which these hints may help to make simpler:

1. Always warm up the crowd with well-known songs before trying out a new one.

2. Provide copies of the words. Use songbooks, mimeographed song sheets, or words on a blackboard or large sheet of paper.

3. Sing the new song through alone or with a small group who already knows it.

4. Let singers try a verse at a time slowly at first. When they master it pick up speed.

5. Musical accompaniment helps—piano, accordion, guitar, harmonica are all good because they can play harmony, not just single melody notes.

6. When they've sung it a time or two, stop—don't make it a music lesson. Go at once into a familiar song.

Use every chance you have to lead and teach songs. Practice on your den, your pack, your family whenever you can. In song leading, as in most musical accomplishments, it takes "do" to get "know-how."

CUB SCOUT PRONUNCIATION GUIDE

There are two words which are often mispronounced in Cub Scout circles—AKELA and WEBELOS. They are properly pronounced:

Akela—Ah-kay´-la

Webelos—Weé-buh-lows

4

HI! THERE, CUB!

Tune: "Hail, Hail, the Gang's All Here"

Hi! Hi! Hi! there, Cub!
We are glad to meet you,
We are glad to greet you.
Hi! Hi! Hi! there, Cub!
You are welcome to our den (pack).

HAIL, HAIL, THE GANG'S ALL HERE

Hail, hail, the gang's all here,
Never mind the weather
Here we are together;
Hail, hail, the gang's all here,
Sure we're glad that you're here, too!

Hail, hail, the gang's all here,
We're a bunch of live ones,
Not a single dead one;
Hail, hail, the gang's all here,
Sure I'm glad that I'm here, too!

CUB SCOUT WELCOME SONG

Tune: "Auld Lang Syne"

We welcome you to our Cub (pack) (den),

We're mighty glad you're here.

We'll start the air reverberating

With a mighty cheer.

We'll sing you in, we'll sing you out,

For you we'll raise a shout.

Hail, Hail, the gang's all here (tonight) (today),

You're welcome to our (pack) (den)!

HOW DO YOU DO?

How do you do, ev-'ry-bo-dy, how do you do? _____ Is there an-y-thing that we can do for you? _____ We are with you to a man, We'll do an-y-thing we can. How do you do, ev-'ry-bo-dy how do you do? ___

WE'RE ALL TOGETHER AGAIN

We're all to - geth - er a -
gain, we're here, we're here. ___ We're
all to - geth - er a - gain, we're here, we're
here. ___ Who knows when we'll be
all to - geth - er a - gain, sing - ing
"All to - geth - er a - gain, we're here."

WE'RE HERE FOR FUN

Tune: "Auld Lang Syne"

We're here for fun right from the start,
So drop your dignity;
Just laugh and sing with all your heart,
And show your loyalty.
May all your troubles be forgot,
Let this night be the best;
Join in the songs we sing tonight,
Be happy with the rest.

THE MORE WE GET TOGETHER

Tune: "Ach Du Lieber Augustine"

The more we get together, together, together,
The more we get together, the happier we'll be.
For your friends are my friends,
And my friends are your friends,
The more we get together, the happier we'll be.

The more we get together, together, together,
The more we get together, the happier we'll be.
For you know that I know,
And I know that you know,
The more we get together, the happier we'll be.

HELLO! HELLO!

Hel - lo,   Hel - lo,   Hel - lo,   Hel - lo,

We're glad to meet you, We're glad to greet you.

Hel - lo,   hel - lo,   hel - lo,   hel - lo!

Divide the singers into four groups, each singing one "Hello" and holding it through to the completion of the full chord, singing the middle part in unison.

WE'RE GLAD TO SEE YOU HERE

Tune: "Farmer in the Dell"

We're glad to see you here,
It gives us joy and cheer.
Sure, it's true, we say to you,
We're glad to see you here.

RECOGNITION SONG

Tune: "Farmer in the Dell"

Our honored guests are here,
Our honored guests are here,
Stand up now and take a bow *(stand)*
Our honored guests are here.

Continue—Den Mothers, leaders, fathers, mothers, sisters, brothers, den chiefs, Cub Scouts, Webelos Scouts, etc.

I LOVE THAT WORD HELLO

Tune: "Auld Lang Syne"

I love to hear that word "hello,"
Wherever I may go.
It's full of friendship and good cheer,
And warms the heart up so.
Hello, hello, hello, hello,
Hello, hello, hello;
Where e'er we meet,
Like friends let's greet
Each other with "hello."

SMILE SONG (S-M-I-L-E)

Tune: "John Brown's Body"

It isn't any trouble just to S-M-I-L-E,

It isn't any trouble just to S-M-I-L-E.

There isn't any trouble, but will vanish
    like a bubble,

If you'll only take the trouble just to
    S-M-I-L-E.

Second verse: It isn't any trouble just to G-R-I-N, Grin, etc.

Third verse: It isn't any trouble just to L-A-U-G-H, etc.

Fourth verse: It isn't any trouble just to HA! HA! HA! HA! HA!, etc.

BE KIND TO YOUR WEB-FOOTED FRIENDS

Tune: "Stars and Stripes Forever"

Be kind to your web-footed friends,

For a duck may be somebody's mother.

Be kind to your friends in the swamp . . .

Where the weather's always damp.

You may think that this is the end,

Well—it is!

THERE WERE THREE JOLLY FISHERMEN

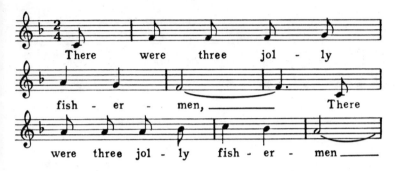

There were three jol - ly fish - er - men, _____ There

were three jol - ly fish - er - men _____

(Group one shouts: Fisher, fisher; group two shouts: Men, men, men.)

_ "Fish - er, fish - er," "Men, men, men."

"Fish - er, fish - er," "Men, men, men." There

were three jol - ly fish - er - men. _____

The first one's name was Abraham,
The first one's name was Abraham,
Abra, Abra; ham, ham, ham, etc.

The second one's name was I-I-saac
The second one's name was I-I-saac
I-I, I-I-; zik, zik, zik, etc.

The third one's name was Ja-a-cob,
The third one's name was Ja-a-cob,
Ja-a, Ja-a; cub, cub, cub, etc.

They all went up to Jericho,
They all went up to Jericho,
Jer-i, Jer-i; cho, cho, cho, etc.

They should have gone to Amsterdam,
They should have gone to Amsterdam,
Amster, Amster; sh, sh, sh, etc.

JOHN JACOB
JINGLEHEIMER SCHMIDT

John   Jac - ob   Jin - gle - heim - er Schmidt,

His name is   my   name too. _____   When-

ev - er we go out the peo-ple al - ways shout,

"John   Jac - ob   Jin - gle - heim - er

Schmidt." Da - da - da - da - da - da - da.

Repeat four times, each time softer, until on the last verse no sound comes out except—Da, da, da, da, da, da.

Music used by permission of Rytvoc Inc., New York.

YANKEE DOODLE

Father and I went down to camp,
Along with Captain Good'in,
And there we saw the men and boys
As thick as hasty puddin'.

Chorus

Yankee Doodle keep it up,
Yankee Doodle dandy,
Mind the music and the step,
And with the girls be handy.

VARIATION

Substitute "Da" for the words and clap out the rhythm.

DIXIE

I wish I was in the land of cotton,
Old times there are not forgotten;
Look away! Look away! Look away! Dixie Land.
In Dixie Land where I was born in,
Early on one frosty mornin',
Look away! Look away! Look away! Dixie Land.

Chorus
Then I wish I was in Dixie, Hooray! Hooray!
In Dixie Land I'll take my stand to live and die in Dixie,
Away, away, away down south in Dixie,
Away, away, away down south in Dixie.

VARIATION
Substitute "Da" for the words and clap out the rhythm.

I HAVE A DOG

Tune: "Reuben, Reuben, I've Been Thinking"

I have a dog, his name is Fido,

I have raised him from a pup.

He can stand upon his hind legs

If you hold his front legs up.

WHERE HAS MY LITTLE DOG GONE?

Oh where, oh where has my little dog gone?

Oh where, oh where can he be?

With his ears cut short and his tail cut long,

Oh where, oh where can he be?

CLEMENTINE

In a cavern, in a canyon,
Excavating for a mine,
Dwelt a miner, forty-niner,
And his daughter, Clementine.

Chorus

Oh my darling, oh my darling, oh my darling Clementine!
Thou art lost and gone forever; dreadful sorry, Clementine.

Light she was, and like a fairy,
And her shoes were number nine,
Herring boxes without topses,
Sandals were for Clementine.

Chorus

Drove she ducklings to the water,
Ev'ry morning just at nine,
Hit her foot against a splinter,
Fell into the foaming brine.

Chorus

Saw her lips above the water,
Blowing bubbles mighty fine,
But alas! I was no swimmer,
So I lost my Clementine.

Chorus

THE CALLIOPE SONG

Divide the pack meeting into four or five groups. Begin with the first group and bring each of the others in one at a time.

1st group sings:	Um-pah-pah
2d group sings:	Um-sss-sss
3d group sings:	Um-peep-peep
4th group (optional) sings:	Um-tweedle-tweedle

Last group sings either the melody of "Daisy, Daisy" *or* "Where Has My Little Dog Gone?" *or* "The More We Get Together"—*found elsewhere in this songbook.*

THE ANIMAL FAIR

I went to the an-i-mal fair, __ The
birds and the beasts were there. __
The old ba-boon by the light of the moon, Was
comb-ing his au-burn hair. __
The fun-ni-est was the monk, __ He
climbed up the el-e-phant's trunk. __
The el-e-phant sneezed and fell on his knees, And
what be-came of the monk? __
The monk, the monk, the monk, the monk.

VARIATIONS

When song is sung through once, a small group may sing the last line over and over as a chant, while rest sing the song a second time.

Other lyrics for the "monkey" line: "The monkey he got drunk, and fell on the elephant's trunk."

DAISY, DAISY

Daisy, Daisy, give me your answer true,
I'm half-crazy all for the love of you.
It won't be a stylish marriage,
I can't afford a carriage;
But you'll look sweet
Upon the seat
Of a bicycle built for two.

OLD MacDONALD HAD A FARM

Old MacDonald had a farm, E-I-E-I-O.
And on this farm, he had some chicks, E-I-E-I-O.
With a chick chick here, and a chick chick there,
Here a chick, there a chick, everywhere a chick chick,*
Old MacDonald had a farm, E-I-E-I-O.

2. Duck—quack quack
3. Turkey—gobble gobble
4. Pig—oink oink
5. Cow—moo moo
6. Mule—hee haw
7. Dog—bow wow
8. Cat—mew mew
9. Ford—rattle rattle

*Repeat third and fourth lines of each verse previously sung.

BINGO

There was a farm-er had a dog And Bing-o was his name-o, B - I - N - G - O, B - I - N - G - O, B - I - N - G - O, And Bing - o was his name - o.

Sing song through six times, the first time just spelling out the name B-I-N-G-O; second time, spell out first four letters and clap the "O"; third time, spell out first three letters and clap the "G" and "O"; etc., until all five letters are clapped out.

(A popular variation on the first line is: "Old MacDonald had a dog and the dog's name was Bingo.")

ALOUETTE

French-Canadian canoe song

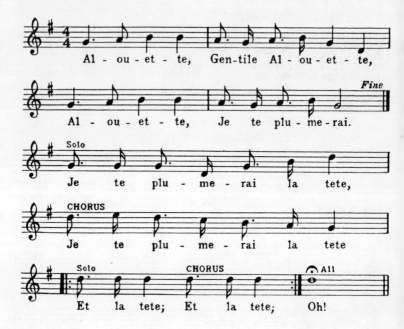

Al - ou - et - te, Gen-tile Al - ou - et - te,

Fine

Al - ou - et - te, Je te plu - me - rai.

Solo

Je te plu - me - rai la tete,

CHORUS

Je te plu - me - rai la tete

Solo   **CHORUS**   **All**

Et la tete; Et la tete; Oh!

2. la bec

3. la nez

4. le cou

5. le dos

6. les ailes

7. les pattes

8. les pieds

ACTION

Each time you sing the melody, add a new word to describe the lark in the measure before the "Oh!" Have everyone repeat this and sing all preceding verses in reverse. Point to the parts as you sing them. Translation: alouette—lark, gentile—pretty, plumer—to pluck (as feathers) or pull, tête—head, bec—beak or bill (mouth), nez—nose, cou—neck, dos—back, ailes—wings, pattes—legs, pieds—feet.

18

RAVIOLI

Tune: "Alouette"

All: Ravioli, I like ravioli.
Ravioli, it's the best for me.

Leader: Have I got it on my chin?

All: Yes, you got it on your chin.

Leader: On my chin?

All: On your chin. OH-h-h-h-h
Ravioli, I like ravioli.
Ravioli, it's the best for me.

(Continue tie, shirt, pants, shoes, floor, walls. Point to the items as each new word is added by the song leader. It is repeated by the chorus and all preceding verses are sung in reverse order.)

All: Ravioli, I like ravioli.
Ravioli, it's the best for me.

Leader: Is it all over?

All: Yes, it's all over.

Leader: Yes, it's all over.

THE GRAND OLD DUKE OF YORK

Tune: "A-Hunting We Will Go"

The grand old Duke of York,
He had ten thousand men.
He marched them up the hill,
  Everyone stands up
And marched them down again.
  Everyone sits down
And when you're up, you're up;
  Everyone up
And when you're down, you're down.
  Everyone down
And when you're only halfway up,
  Everyone halfway up
You're neither up nor down.
  All up   All down

Repeat several times, each time getting faster.

SHE'LL BE COMIN' 'ROUND THE MOUNTAIN

With motions and sound effects

1. She'll be comin' 'round the mountain when she comes,
    Toot, toot!

Motion for pulling whistle cord

>   She'll be comin' 'round the mountain when she comes,
>   Toot, toot!

Same motion

>   She'll be comin' 'round the mountain,
>   She'll be comin' 'round the mountain,
>   She'll be comin' 'round the mountain when she comes,
>   Toot, toot!

Same motion

2. She'll be drivin' six white horses when she comes,
    Whoa, back!

Pull back on reins

3. And we'll all go out to meet her when she comes,
    Hi, Babe!

Wave hand

4. And we'll kill the old red rooster when she comes,
    Hack, hack!

Chop wrist with side of hand

5. And we'll all have chicken 'n' dumplings when she comes,
    Yum, yum!

Rub tummy

DIRECTIONS
At the end of each verse, repeat in reverse order the sounds and motions of the preceding verses.

MY HAT, IT HAS THREE CORNERS

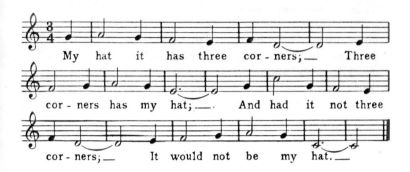

My hat it has three cor-ners;— Three cor-ners has my hat;— And had it not three cor-ners;— It would not be my hat.—

MOTIONS

My—point to yourself
Hat—tap your head
Three—hold up three fingers
Corners—form with your hands

Sing through first time with words only.
Sing through second time with both words and motions.
Substitute motions for words the third time through.

SMILE AWHILE

Tune: "Till We Meet Again"

Smile awhile and give your face a rest.
   Make a big smile
Stretch awhile and ease your weary chest.
   Stretch arms
Reach your hands up toward the sky.
   Raise hands above head
While you watch them with your eyes.
   Look up and watch hands
Jump awhile and shake a leg, Sir.
   Jump once, then shake leg
Now step forward, backward as you were.
   Do as words say
Then reach right out to someone near.
   Do as words say
Shake his hand and smile.
   Do as words say

JOHN BROWN'S BABY

Tune: "John Brown's Body"

John Brown's baby had a cold upon its chest,
John Brown's baby had a cold upon its chest,
John Brown's baby had a cold upon its chest,
And they rubbed it up with camphorated oil.

MOTIONS

1st time—sing straight through

2d time—omit singing "baby" and substitute motion of rocking baby

3d time—omit "cold" and substitute a coughing sound

4th time—same as third only substitute striking chest for "chest"

5th time—same as fourth only omit last line and rub chest

LITTLE PETER RABBIT

Tune: "John Brown's Body"

Little Peter Rabbit had a flea upon his ear.
Little Peter Rabbit had a flea upon his ear.
Little Peter Rabbit had a flea upon his ear,
And he flipped the little flea away.

ACTION

1st time—sing straight through

2d time—omit singing "Peter Rabbit" and substitute rabbit ears using forefingers of hands against forehead

3d time—same as second time; then omit "flea" and substitute scratching your ear

4th time—same as third; then omit "ear" and point forefinger at ear

5th time—same as fourth; then omit "flipped" and substitute flipping of earlobe with fingers

6th time—same as fifth; then omit "away" and substitute flapping motions of both arms as if you're flying

22

THROW IT OUT THE WINDOW

Old Moth-er Hub-bard went to the cup-board To get her poor dog a bone. When she got there the cup-board was bare, So she threw it out the win-dow, the win-dow, the win-dow; She threw it out the win-dow. When she got there _ the cup - board was bare, So she threw it out the win - dow. _____

Mary had a little lamb,
Its fleece was white as snow
And everywhere that Mary went
She threw it out the window, the window, (the window,)
She threw it out the window.
And everywhere that Mary went

(The fourth line of the nursery rhyme is always repeated here.)

She threw it out the window.

Divide the group into two or more teams. One team starts by singing a Mother Goose rhyme. Instead of singing the last line, however, the players substitute the words, "she threw it out the window" (motion throw-

(continued on next page)

ing with arms). As soon as one team finishes, another starts. A team is eliminated if it fails to start singing as soon as its turn comes. Suggested rhymes include "Little Jack Horner," "Old King Cole," "Little Bo Peep," "Little Miss Muffet," "Jack and Jill," etc.

IF YOU'RE HAPPY

2d verse

If you're happy and you know it, stamp your feet.
(stamp-stamp)

3d verse

If you're happy and you know it, shout "Amen."
("Amen")

4th verse

If you're happy and you know it, do all three.
(clap-clap) (stamp-stamp) ("Amen")

ITSY BITSY SPIDER

Moderately

It - sy bit - sy spi - der climb'd up the wat - er spout, Down came the rain, and washed the spi - der out, Out came the sun and dried up all the rain, And the it - sy bit - sy spi - der climb'd up the spout a-gain.

ACTION

To imitate spider make forefingers and thumbs climb upward, make "raining" downward actions with hands, form a "sun" with hands in front, then climb again.

DO YOUR EARS HANG LOW?

Tune: "Turkey in the Straw"

Do your ears hang low
Do they wobble to and fro
Can you tie them in a knot
Can you tie them in a bow
Can you throw them o'er your shoulder,
Like a Continental soldier?
Do your ears — hang — low?

25

HEAD AND SHOULDERS, KNEES AND TOES

Tune: "There Is a Tavern in the Town"

Head and shoulders, knees and toes, knees and toes,
Head and shoulders, knees and toes, knees and toes,
Eyes and ears and mouth and nose,
Head and shoulders, knees and toes, knees and toes.

DIRECTIONS

1st time—sing straight through, touching parts of the body

2d time—omit singing "head" and touch it

3d time—omit singing "shoulders" and touch them

4th time—omit singing "knees" and touch them

5th time—omit singing "toes" and touch them

Touch each part of your body as you mention it in the song. For example, head—put your hands on your head. Each time you start a new verse, drop another word, but keep the motion. Extra verses may be added to include all parts of body mentioned.

MY BONNIE

My Bonnie lies over the ocean,

My Bonnie lies over the sea.

My Bonnie lies over the ocean,

Oh, bring back my Bonnie to me.

Bring back, bring back,

Oh, bring back my Bonnie to me, to me.

Bring back, bring back,

Oh, bring back my Bonnie to me.

ACTION VERSION

Stand up on the first word with a "b" in it then sit down on the next "b" and so on with each word with a "b" in it. The whole group should end the song sitting down!

ONE FINGER, ONE THUMB

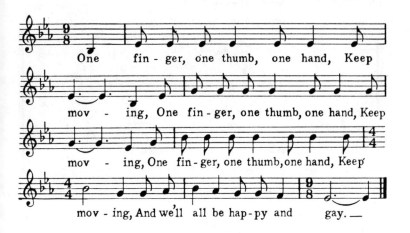

2. One finger, one thumb, one hand, two hands;
   Keep moving.

Repeat three times

   And we'll all be happy and gay.

Add in turn:

3. One arm

4. Two arms

5. One leg

6. Two legs

7. Stand up—sit down

NOTE

Words are accompanied by motions with finger, thumb, hand, raising arms, stamping foot, standing-up and sitting-down actions.

THREE BLIND MICE

Four-Part Round

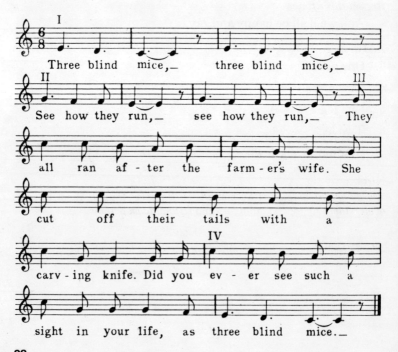

I
Three blind mice,— three blind mice,—

II
See how they run,— see how they run,— They

III
all ran af - ter the farm - er's wife. She

cut off their tails with a

IV
carv - ing knife. Did you ev - er see such a

sight in your life, as three blind mice.—

ARE YOU SLEEPING?

Four-Part Round

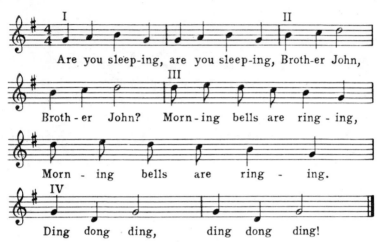

Are you sleep-ing, are you sleep-ing, Broth-er John,
Broth - er John? Morn-ing bells are ring - ing,
Morn - ing bells are ring - ing.
Ding dong ding, ding dong ding!

SANTA'S COMING

Tune: "Are You Sleeping?"

Santa's coming, Santa's coming,
Hear the bells, hear the bells.
You had better be good, you had better be good,
Little boy, little boy.

HI HO! NOBODY HOME

Hi, ho no - bod - y home,
meat nor drink, nor mon - ey have I none
Yet will I be mer - - - r - y.

ROW, ROW, ROW YOUR BOAT

Four-Part Round

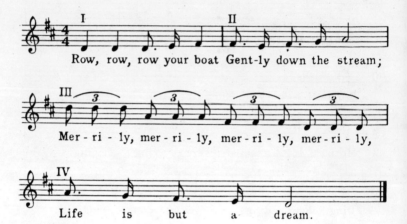

Row, row, row your boat Gent-ly down the stream;

Mer - ri - ly, mer - ri - ly, mer - ri - ly, mer - ri - ly,

Life is but a dream.

LITTLE TOMMY TINKER

Four-Part Round

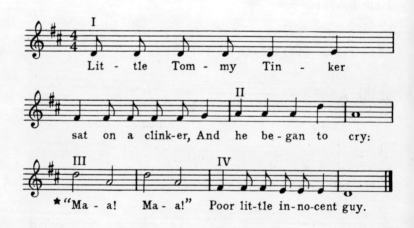

Lit - tle Tom - my Tin - ker

sat on a clink-er, And he be-gan to cry:

★ "Ma - a! Ma - a!" Poor lit-tle in-no-cent guy.

★ *Stand up while singing "Ma-a! Ma-a!" then sit down again.*

30

SWEETLY SINGS THE DONKEY

Three-Part Round

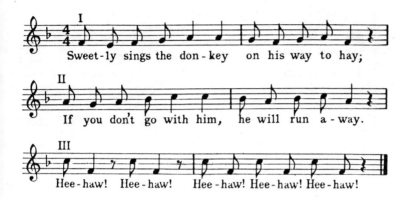

I
Sweet-ly sings the don-key on his way to hay;

II
If you don't go with him, he will run a-way.

III
Hee-haw! Hee-haw! Hee-haw! Hee-haw! Hee-haw!

When saying "Hee-haw," put your hands at head and flop them.

DOWN BY THE STATION

Four-Part Round

I
Down by the sta-tion ear-ly in the morn-ing,

II
See the lit-tle puf-fer bil-lies all in a row.

III
See the en-gine driv-er turn the lit-tle han-dle.

IV
Chug! Chug! Whoo! Whoo! Off they go!

Cub Scout Songs

CUB SCOUT BOOSTER SONG

Tune: "Put on Your Old Gray Bonnet"

Pull off your coat and collar,
Get to work and push and holler,
And we'll push Cub Scouting to the top.
Every booster boostin',
Not a rooster roostin',
We will never, never stop.

CUB SCOUT ADVANCEMENT SONG

Tune: "Farmer in the Dell"

1. A-Cubbing we will go, a-Cubbing we will go,
Chorus
    Hi, ho, the daireo, a-Cubbing we will go.
2. The Bobcat makes a Wolf, the Bobcat makes a Wolf,
Chorus
3. The Wolf Cub makes a Bear, the Wolf Cub makes a Bear,
Chorus
4. Then next is We-be-los, then next is We-be-los,
Chorus
5. The Webelos makes a Scout, the Webelos makes a Scout,
Chorus
6. A-Scouting we will go, a-Scouting we will go,
    Hi, ho, the daireo, a-Scouting we will go.
    Ta, ta, ta, ta, ta, ta, ta, ta, ta, a-Scouting we will go.
    Ta, ta, ta, ta, ta, ta, ta, ta, ta, a-Scouting we will go.

OLD AKELA HAD A PACK

Tune: "Old MacDonald Had a Farm"

1
Old Akela had a pack, E-I-E-I-O.
And in this pack he had some dens, E-I-E-I-O.
With a Den 1 here, and a Den 2 there;
Here a den, there a den,
Everywhere a happy den,
Old Akela had a pack, E-I-E-I-O.

2
And for these dens he had some chiefs, E-I-E-I-O.
(With a den chief here, and a den chief there)

3
And in these dens he had some Cubs, E-I-E-I-O.
(With a Cub Scout here ———)

4
And for these dens he had some moms, E-I-E-I-O.
(With a den mom here ———)

5
And for these dens he had some dads, E-I-E-I-O.
With a den dad here, and a den dad there;
Here a dad, there a dad,
Everywhere a den dad;
With a den mom here, and a den mom there;
Here a mom, there a mom,
Everywhere a den mom;
With a Cub Scout here, and a Cub Scout there;
Here a Scout, there a Scout,
Everywhere a Cub Scout;
With a den chief here, and a den chief there;
Here a chief, there a chief,
Everywhere a den chief;
With a Den 1 here, and a Den 2 there;
Here a den, there a den,
Everywhere a happy den;
Old Akela had a pack, E-I-E-I-O.

THIS LITTLE CUBBING LIGHT

(This lit-tle Cub-bing light of mine) I'm goin' to let it shine. (This lit-tle Cub-bing light of mine) I'm goin' to let it shine. (This lit-tle Cub-bing light of mine) I'm goin' to let it shine, Let it shine all the time, Let it shine.

2. All around the neighborhood

3. Hide it under a bushel—No!

4. Don't you "pfft" my little light out

ACTION

1. *Hold right forefinger up like a candle.*

2. *Move finger around in a square, and back to starting point.*

3. *Place cupped left hand over the "light," then withdraw it quickly and shout, "NO!"*

4. *In saying "pfft," pretend to blow the light out.*

I'VE GOT THAT CUB SCOUT SPIRIT

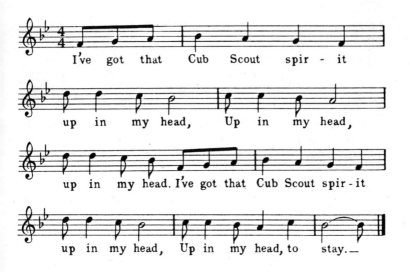

(Replace "head" with other words in last four verses.)

I've got that Cub Scout spirit
Deep in my heart, etc.

(Continue as in first verse.)
I've got that Cub Scout spirit
Down in my feet, etc.

I've got that Cub Scout spirit
All over me, etc.

I've got that Cub Scout spirit
Up in my head,
Deep in my heart,
Down in my feet,
I've got that Cub Scout spirit
All over me,
All over me, to stay.

MOTION
For more spirit, you can point to each part of body as you sing.

THE PROMISE AND LAW

Tune: "Auld Lang Syne"

I promise to do my best to do
My duty to God
And to my country;
To be square, and
Obey the Law of the Pack.
The Cub Scout follows Akela.
The Cub Scout helps the pack go.
The pack helps the Cub Scout grow.
The Cub Scout gives goodwill.

CUBS WHISTLE
WHILE THEY WORK

Tune: "Whistle While You Work"

Cubs whistle while they work!

Whistle

They pitch right in, and laugh, and grin,
And whistle while they work.

Cubs hum a merry tune!

Hum

They hum all day at work and play,
They hum a merry tune.

Before they join the Scouts,
They have to know the rule
Of being courteous and kind
In both their home and school.

Cubs whistle while they work,

Whistle

They do their bit, they never quit,
Cubs whistle while they work.

CUB SCOUT MARCHING SONG

Tune: "This Old Man"

This young Cub, number one,
He sure likes to get things done.

Chorus (Repeat after each stanza.)

With a knick knack paddy wack
Give a Cub a chore
This he'll do and ask for more.

This young Cub, number two,
He will do odd jobs for you.

This young Cub, number three,
Full of humor, full of glee.

This young Cub, number four,
Follows rules and knows the score.

This young Cub, number five,
He has courage, he has drive.

This young Cub, number six,
He'll make things with ropes and sticks.

This young Cub, number seven,
Becomes a Boy Scout at eleven.

This young Cub, number eight,
Gives goodwill that sure does rate.

This young Cub, number nine,
He's so pleasant all the time.

This young Cub, number ten,
Sings the chorus once again.

THE (WOLF) (BEAR) (WEB'LO) WENT OVER THE MOUNTAIN

Tune: "For He's a Jolly Good Fellow"

The wolf went over the mountain,
The wolf went over the mountain,
The wolf went over the mountain,
To see what he could see.

And all that he could see,
And all that he could see,
Was the other side of the mountain,
The other side of the mountain,
The other side of the mountain,
Was all that he could see.

Sing first using "Wolf"—then "Bear" and finally "Web'lo."

CUBBING ALONG TOGETHER

Tune: "Marching Along Together"

Cubbing along together, sharing every smile and tear.
Cubbing along together, whistling till the skies are clear.
Singing along the highway, over the Cub Scout trail,
Without a bugle, without a drum,
We're Cub Scout pioneers.
Oh, rum de diddle dee, here we come,
Just hear those happy cheers.
So! Cubbing along together, hiking along the Cub Scout trail.

Cubbing along together, working on Akela's dream.
Cubbing along together, working as a well-knit team.
Singing along the highway, keeping the vision wide.
A happy song and a Cub Scout smile,
Will help us on our way;
Our Promise true, and our Law so bright,
To guide us day by day.
So! Cubbing along together, life is wonderful side by side.

Music copyrighted by Robbins Music Co., 799 7th Avenue, New York. Available from your local dealer. Adaptation used by permission.

CUBBING IN THE MORNING

Tune: "Sugartime"

Cubbing in the morning, Cubbing in the evening,
Cubbing at any time.
You'll find fun and laughter, in Cubbing all the time.
Cubbing in the morning, Cubbing in the evening,
Cubbing at any time.
It's fun we're after, in Cubbing all the time.
Put your left hand out there, extend that thumb along,
Make that living circle, and sing our Cubbing song.
Cubbing in the morning, Cubbing in the evening,
Cubbing at any time.
Shout it to the rafters and Cub along all the time.

HAIL TO CUBBING

Tune: "On Wisconsin"

Hail to Cubbing! Hail to Cubbing!
Best game of them all.
We're a bunch of jolly Cub Scouts,
Listen to our call—
Rah! Rah! Rah!
Ever onward, ever forward—
Bringing fun to all!
Here's to the game of Cubbing,
Best of all!

Webelos Songs

I'M HAPPY WHEN I'M HIKING

English Hiking Song

Tramp, tramp, tramp, tramp, tramp, tramp, tramp, tramp.

I'm hap-py when I'm hik - ing, pack up-on my

back. I'm hap-py when I'm hik-ing off the beat-en

track. Out in the o-pen coun-try, that's the place for

me. With a true Scout-ing friend To the jour-ney's end,

ten, twen-ty, thir - ty, for - ty, fif - ty miles a

day. Tramp, tramp, tramp. *(Repeat tramp to end.)*

WE'LL BE LOYAL SCOUTS

Tune: "Aura Lee"

On our ho-nor we've been true   To the gold and

blue. ___   We've been Cub Scouts for two years,

CHORUS

Now we're We-be-los.   We-be-los, We-be-los,

We're the ten-year-olds.   We'll be lo-yal

Scouts next year, The tribe of We-be-los.

Crafts and badges fill our days
And Boy Scouting ways.
We play sports, have camp-outs, too,
For we're Webelos.

Chorus

We look forward to Boy Scouts
In the years ahead,
While we work on our award
Called the Webelos.

Chorus

Soon we'll graduate from Cubs
And we'll cross the bridge
To Boy Scouting's happy trails
And leave Webelos.

SCOUTING WE GO

Verse Tune: "I've Been Workin' on the Railroad"

I was dreaming of a campfire
Burning clear and bright;
Glistening stars were out above me,
Twas on a summer's night.
I was dreaming that my comrades
All were camping too;
Then I woke and looked around me,
And say—that dream was true.

Scout-ing we go, Scout-ing we go, Sun-lit trails and lands where wa-ters flow By the camp fire's friend-ly, flam-ing glow. Scout-ing we go, Scout-ing we go.

WE'RE ON THE UPWARD TRAIL

We're on the up-ward trail, We're on the up-ward trail, Sing-ing as we go Scout - ing bound. We're on the up - ward trail, We're on the up-ward trail, Sing-ing, sing-ing, ev -'ry - bo - dy sing-ing, Scout - ing bound.

NOTE

This song may be sung by two groups as a "round." The second group starts as the first group reaches the word "trail" in the second measure, skips the measure containing "ev'rybody singing," and joins the first group on the final "Scouting bound."

THE HAPPY WANDERER

Antonia Ridge   Friedn W. Möller

I love to go a-wander-ing, A-long the
moun-tain track,—And as I go, I love to
sing, My knap-sack on my back.—Val-de
ri—Val-de ra—Val-de ra—Val-de
ha ha ha ha ha ha Val-de ri,—Val-de
ra. My knap-sack on my back.

I love to wander by the stream
    That dances in the sun,
So joyously it calls to me,
    "Come! Join my happy song!"

I wave my hat to all I meet,
    And they wave back to me,
And blackbirds call so loud and sweet
    From ev'ry green-wood tree.

High overhead, the skylarks wing,
    They never rest at home
But just like me, they love to sing,
    As o'er the world we roam.

Oh, may I go awandering
    Until the day I die!
Oh, may I always laugh and sing.
Beneath God's clear blue sky!

By special permission of the Sam Fox Publishing Company, Inc.

Theme Songs

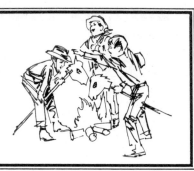

I'VE BEEN WORKIN' ON THE RAILROAD

I've been workin' on the railroad
All the live-long day.
I've been workin' on the railroad,
Just to pass the time away.
Can't you hear the whistle blowing?
Rise up so early in the morn.
Can't you hear the captain shouting,
"Dinah, blow your horn!"

Dinah won't you blow, Dinah won't you blow,
Dinah won't you blow your horn, your horn!
Dinah won't you blow, Dinah won't you blow,
Dinah won't you blow your horn!

TEN LITTLE INDIANS

One little, two little, three little Indians,
Four little, five little, six little Indians,
Seven little, eight little, nine little Indians;
Ten little Indian boys.

Sing song through once and then reverse the words on the next time through—Ten little, nine little, eight little Indians, and so on to one little Indian boy. For extra excitement, you can give a war whoop after the second verse.

HOME ON THE RANGE

How often at night when the heavens are bright,
With the light from the glittering stars,
Have I stood here amazed and asked as I gazed,
If their glory exceeds that of ours.

GIT ALONG, LITTLE DOGIES

Sing rhythmically to the swing of riding a horse—don't drag it.

As I was a-walk-ing one morn-ing for pleas-ure,

I spied a cow-punch-er a-rid-ing a-long;

His hat was throwed back and his spurs was a-jin-gling,

And as he ap-proached he was sing-ing this song:

CHORUS

Whoop-ee ti yi yo,— git a-long, lit-tle do-gies,

It's your mis-for-tune and none of my own,

Whoop-ee ti yi yo,— git a-long, lit tle do-gies,

You know that Wy-o-ming will be your new home.

It's whooping and yelling and driving the dogies,
And oh, how I wish you would only git on.
It's whooping and punching, git on, little dogies,
You know that Wyoming will be your new home.
Chorus

47

THE COWBOY'S SWEET BYE AND BYE

Tune: "My Bonnie"

Last night as I lay on the prairie
And gazed at the stars in the skies,
I wondered if ever a cowboy
Could drift to that sweet bye and bye.

Chorus

Roll on, roll on,
Roll on little dogies,
Roll on, roll on,
Roll on, roll on,
Roll on little dogies, roll on.

The road to that bright heavenly region
Is a dim narrow trail, so they say,
But the road that leads down to perdition
Is posted and blazed all the way.

Chorus

They speak of another Great Owner
Who's never o'erstocked, so they say,
But who always makes room for the sinner
Who drifts from the straight narrow way.

Chorus

They tell of another great roundup,
Where cowboys like dogies will stand,
To be marked by the Riders of Judgment,
Who are posted and know every brand.

Chorus

Sing the "roll" of the chorus as "ro-o-oll." Dogies mean cattle. This song is sung as cowboys drive their cattle in the roundup.

PINEWOOD DERBY SONG

Tune: "Camptown Races"

Cub Scouts all join in the song,
Doo-dah, doo-dah!
Pine car track is mighty long,
Oh, doo-dah day!

Chorus

Going to run so fast,
Going to get ahead.
Bet my money on a blue pine car,
Somebody bet on the red.

Red cars, blue cars, green, and gray,
Doo-dah, doo-dah!
Running on the track today,
Oh, doo-dah day!

Chorus

Pinewood cars have lots of class,
Doo-dah, doo-dah!
Even though they don't use gas,
Oh, doo-dah day!

Chorus

They're the pride of all the lads,
Doo-dah, doo-dah!
Built by Cub Scouts and their dads,
Oh, doo-dah day!

Chorus

SPACE DERBY SONG

Tune: "Camptown Races"

Cub Scouts all join in the song,
Doo-dah, doo-dah!
Spaceship wire is mighty long,
Oh, doo-dah day!

Chorus

Going to fly so fast,
Going to get ahead,
Bet my money on a blue spaceship,
Somebody bet on the red.

Spaceships—red, blue, green, and gray,
Doo-dah, doo-dah!
Running on the wire today,
Oh, doo-dah day!

Chorus

Spaceships have a lot of speed,
Doo-dah, doo-dah!
Rubber bands are all they need,
Oh, doo-dah day!

Chorus

They're the pride of all the lads,
Doo-dah, doo-dah!
Built by Cub Scouts and their dads,
Oh, doo-dah day!

Chorus

TRAIN SONG

Tune: "Yankee Doodle"

I met an engine on a hill,
All hot and broken-hearted,
And this is what he said to me
As up the hill he started.

Slowly

I think I can, I think I can,
At any rate, I'll try.
I think I can, I think I can,
At any rate, I'll try.

Slowly

A-choo choo choo, a-choo choo choo,
A-choo choo choo choo choo;
A-choo choo choo, a-choo choo choo,
A-choo choo choo choo choo.

He reached the top, and looking back
To where he stood and doubted,
He started on the downward track
And this is what he shouted:

Quickly

I knew I could, I knew I could,
I never should have doubted.
I knew I could, I knew I could,
I never should have doubted.

THE CIRCUS COMES TO TOWN

Tune: "When Johnny Comes Marching Home"

The Cub Scout circus comes to town,
Hurrah! Hurrah!
The elephants, monkeys, and the clowns,
Hurrah! Hurrah!
The big brass band, the merry-go-round,
The midway acts with lots of sound!
And we'll all be there,
When the circus comes to town.

Repeat

THE STATE SONG

Tune: "Our Boys Will Shine Tonight"

Oh, what did Tenna-see, boys, what did Tenna-see?
(Tennessee)
Sing three times

I ask you men, as a personal friend,
What did Tenna-see?

She saw what Arkin-saw, boys, she saw what Arkin-saw.
(Arkansas)
Sing three times

I'll tell you then as a personal friend,
She saw what Arkin-saw.

Similarly

Where has Ora-gone, boys? *(Oregon)*
She's taking Okla-home, boys. *(Oklahoma)*
How did Wiscon-sin, boys? *(Wisconsin)*
She stole a New-brass-key, boys. *(Nebraska)*
What did Della-ware, boys? *(Delaware)*
She wore a New Jersey, boys. *(New Jersey)*
What did Io-weigh, boys? *(Iowa)*
She weighed a Washing-ton, boys. *(Washington)*
Where did Ida-hoe, boys? *(Idaho)*
She hoed in Merry-land, boys. *(Maryland)*
What did Missy-sip, boys? *(Mississippi)*
She sipped her Mini-soda, boys. *(Minnesota)*
What did Connie-cut, boys? *(Connecticut)*
She cut her shaggy Mane, boys. *(Maine)*
What did Ohi-owe, boys? *(Ohio)*
She owed her Taxes, boys. *(Texas)*
How did Flora-die, boys? *(Florida)*
She died of Misery, boys. *(Missouri)*

A-GARDENING WE WILL GO

Tune: "Farmer in the Dell"

A-gardening we will go, a-gardening we will go,
Hi, ki, Akela, the Cub Scouts are not slow.

Chorus—after each verse

Let's garden all the more, let's garden all the more,
Hi, ki, Akela, we'll garden more and more.

Den 1—Preparing

We rake and spade and plow, we rake and spade and plow,
Hi, ki, Akela, we're getting somewhere now.

Den 2—Planting

We water, plant, and hoe, we water, plant and hoe,
Hi, ki, Akela, every Tom and Jack and Joe.

Den 3—Cultivating

We weed and weed and weed, we weed and weed and weed,
Hi, ki, Akela, we must protect our seed.

Den 4—Debugging

We spray and kill and pick, we spray and kill and pick,
Hi, ki, Akela, we'll make those bugs all sick.

Den 5—Harvesting

We harvest all our food, we harvest all our food,
Hi, ki, Akela, we've done the best we could.

ACTION

Dens can act out each verse if desired as words describe.

Patriotic Songs

THE STAR-SPANGLED BANNER

O say, can you see, by the dawn's early light,

What so proudly we hail'd at the twilight's last gleaming,

Whose broad stripes and bright stars, through the perilous fight,

O'er the ramparts we watched were so gallantly streaming?

And the rockets' red glare, the bombs bursting in air,

Gave proof through the night that our flag was still there;

O say, does that star-spangled banner yet wave,

O'er the land of the free, and the home of the brave?

O, thus be it ever when freemen shall stand,

Between their lov'd homes and the war's desolation,

Blest with vict'ry and peace, may the heav'n-rescued land,

Praise the Power that hath made and preserved us a nation.

Then conquer we must, when our cause it is just,

And this be our motto, "In God is our trust,"

And the star-spangled banner in triumph shall wave,

O'er the land of the free, and the home of the brave.

—Francis Scott Key

AMERICA, THE BEAUTIFUL

O beautiful for spacious skies,
For amber waves of grain,
For purple mountain majesties
Above the fruited plain!
America! America! God shed His grace on thee
And crown thy good with brotherhood
From sea to shining sea!

O beautiful for patriot dream
That sees beyond the years,
Thine alabaster cities gleam,
Undimmed by human tears!
America! America! God shed His grace on thee
And crown thy good with brotherhood
From sea to shining sea!

—Katherine Lee Bates

COLUMBIA, THE GEM OF THE OCEAN

O Columbia, the gem of the ocean,
The home of the brave and the free,
The shrine of each patriot's devotion,
A world offers homage to thee.
Thy mandates make heroes assemble,
When Liberty's form stands in view;
Thy banners make tyranny tremble,
When borne by the red, white, and blue!

Chorus

When borne by the red, white, and blue!
When borne by the red, white, and blue!
Thy banners make tyranny tremble,
When borne by the red, white, and blue!

—Thomas A. Becket

AMERICA

My country! 'tis of thee,
Sweet land of liberty,
Of thee I sing;
Land where my fathers died,
Land of the pilgrims' pride,
From ev'ry mountain side
Let freedom ring.

Our fathers' God, to Thee,
Author of Liberty,
To Thee we sing;
Long may our land be bright
With freedom's holy light;
Protect us by Thy might,
Great God, our King.

—Rev. Samuel F. Smith

GOD BLESS AMERICA

God bless America

Land that I love,

Stand beside her and guide her

Through the night with a light from above.

From the mountains, to the prairies,

To the oceans, white with foam,

God bless America, my home sweet home,

God bless America, my home sweet home.

BATTLE-HYMN OF THE REPUBLIC

Mine eyes have seen the glory of the coming of the Lord;

He is trampling out the vintage where the grapes of wrath are
  stored;

He hath loosed the fateful lightning of his terrible swift sword.

His truth is marching on.

Chorus

Glory, glory! Hallelujah!

Glory, glory! Hallelujah!

Glory, glory! Hallelujah!

His truth is marching on.

—Julia Ward Howe

THIS LAND IS YOUR LAND

Woody Guthrie   Gospel Tune

This land is your land—this land is my land—
From Cal-i-for-nia—to the New York Is-land,
From the red-wood for-est—to the Gulf Stream wa-ters,
This land was made for you and me.——

As I went walking that ribbon of highway
I saw above me that endless skyway,
I saw below me that golden valley,
This land was made for you and me.

I roamed and rambled, and I followed my footsteps,
To the sparkling sands of her diamond deserts,
All around me a voice was sounding,
This land was made for you and me.

When the sun came shining, then I was strolling,
And the wheat fields waving, and the dust clouds rolling,
A voice was chanting as the fog was lifting,
This land was made for you and me.

Closing Songs

GOOD NIGHT, CUB SCOUTS

Tune: "Good Night, Ladies"

Good night, Cub Scouts.
Good night, Cub Scouts.
Good night, Cub Scouts.
We're going to leave you now.

Chorus
Merrily, we Cub along, Cub along, Cub along.
Merrily, we Cub along
Up the Cub Scout trail.

Sweet dreams, Cub Scouts.
Sweet dreams, Cub Scouts.
Sweet dreams, Cub Scouts,
We're going to leave you now.

GOOD NIGHT, CUBBERS

Tune: "Good Night, Ladies"

Good night, Cubbers.
Good night, Cubbers.
Good night, Cubbers.
We'll see you all next month.
Chorus

PARTING SONG

Tune: "Now the Day Is Over"

Cubs, it's time we're parting
From our cozy den.
Where we have thought over
Things that make us men.

Let us ask Akela
To help us every day,
While we try our hardest
To do our best always.

TAPS

Day is done,
Gone the sun,
From the lake,
From the hills,
From the sky;
All is well, safely rest,
God is nigh.

Fading light
Dims the sight,
And a star
Gems the sky,
Gleaming bright;
From afar, drawing nigh,
Falls the night.

NOTE

To fix the sequence of first verse in mind remember the order the sun disappears—lake, hills, sky.

BLESS OUR CUB SCOUTS

Tune: "Bless This House"

Bless our Cub Scouts, Lord we pray,
Keep them healthy, all the day.
Let them know their Cub Scout sign,
Have it always on their mind.
If they do, we promise them,
They'll become good future men.
Hear their prayers at night and day,
Guide them, Lord, along their way.

SCOUT'S GOOD-NIGHT SONG

Tune: "Santa Lucia"

Footsteps on distant trail
Campward are bending;
Birch fire and bubbling stew
Rich odors sending;
Here is your heart's desire,
Rest when your feet shall tire;
Open air, pals, food, and fire;
Joys never ending.

Campfires are burning low,
No longer leaping;
Scouts are joining in their evening song,
Shadows come creeping;
Sun sinks below the west,
Good-night and may you rest,
Blankets warm and by soft sounds caressed;
Scouts all are sleeping.

SCOUT VESPER SONG

Tune: "Tannenbaum"

Softly falls the light of day,
While our campfire fades away.
Silently each Scout should ask:
"Have I done my daily task?
Have I kept my honor bright?
Can I guiltless sleep tonight?
Have I done and have I dared
Everything to be prepared?"

THE SCOUT BENEDICTION

CUB SCOUT PRAYER

Tune: "Tannenbaum"

Lord, in this evening hour I pray
For strength to do my best each day.
Draw near to me that I may see
The kind of Cub that I should be.

In serving others, let me see
That I am only serving Thee.
Bless me, oh Lord, in Thy great love,
That I may be a better Cub.

—Submitted by Helen Allen, Den Mother, Portland, Oreg.

TELL ME WHY

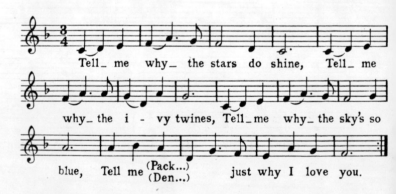

Tell me why the stars do shine, Tell me why the ivy twines, Tell me why the sky's so blue, Tell me (Pack...) (Den...) just why I love you.

Because God made the stars to shine,
Because God made the ivy twine,
Because God made the skies so blue,
Dear old (Pack) (Den) .... that's why I love you!

NOTE
Insert den or pack number in blank space.

INDEX